Baseball Legends

Hank Aaron
Grover Cleveland Alexander
Ernie Banks
Johnny Bench
Yogi Berra
Roy Campanella
Roberto Clemente
Ty Cobb
Dizzy Dean
Joe DiMaggio
Bob Feller
Jimmie Foxx
Lou Gehrig
Bob Gibson
Rogers Hornsby
Reggie Jackson
Shoeless Joe Jackson
Walter Johnson
Sandy Koufax
Mickey Mantle
Christy Mathewson
Willie Mays
Stan Musial
Satchel Paige
Brooks Robinson
Frank Robinson
Jackie Robinson
Pete Rose
Babe Ruth
Nolan Ryan
Mike Schmidt
Tom Seaver
Duke Snider
Warren Spahn
Willie Stargell
Casey Stengel
Honus Wagner
Ted Williams
Carl Yastrzemski
Cy Young

NEWFIELD
PUBLICATIONS

BASEBALL LEGENDS

TOM SEAVER

Norman L. Macht

Introduction by
Jim Murray

———

Senior Consultant
Earl Weaver

CHELSEA HOUSE PUBLISHERS
New York • Philadelphia

Published by arrangement with
Chelsea House Publishers.
Newfield Publications is a federally
registered trademark of Newfield
Publications, Inc.

CHELSEA HOUSE PUBLISHERS

Editorial Director: Richard Rennert
Executive Managing Editor: Karyn Gullen Browne
Copy Chief: Robin James
Picture Editor: Adrian G. Allen
Art Director: Robert Mitchell
Manufacturing Director: Gerald Levine
Production Coordinator: Marie Claire Cebrián-Ume

Baseball Legends
Senior Editor: Philip Koslow

Staff for TOM SEAVER
Editorial Assistant: Kelsey Goss
Designer: M. Cambraia Magalhães
Picture Researcher: Alan Gottlieb
Cover Illustration: Daniel O'Leary

Library of Congress Cataloging-in-Publication Data

Macht, Norman L. (Norman Lee), 1929–
Tom Seaver / Norman L. Macht
p. cm.—(Baseball legends)
Includes bibliographical references (p.) and index.
Summary: A biography of the major league pitcher who played an important role in helping
the New York Mets win the 1969 World Championship.
ISBN 0-7910-1951-9
1. Seaver, Tom, 1944–   —Juvenile literature. 2. Pitchers (Baseball)—United States —Biography—
Juvenile literature. [1. Seaver, Tom, 1944– . 2. Baseball players.]
I. Title. II. Series.
GV865.S4M33 1994   91-17289
796.357'22'092—dc20   CIP
[B]   AC

CONTENTS

WHAT MAKES A STAR

Jim Murray

No one has ever been able to explain to me the mysterious alchemy that makes one man a .350 hitter and another player, more or less identical in physical makeup, hard put to hit .200. You look at an Al Kaline, who played with the Detroit Tigers from 1953 to 1974. He was pale, stringy, almost poetic-looking. He always seemed to be struggling against a bad case of mononucleosis. But with a bat in his hands, he was King Kong. During his career, he hit 399 home runs, rapped out 3,007 hits, and compiled a .297 batting average.

Form isn't the reason. The first time anybody saw Roberto Clemente step into the batter's box for the Pittsburgh Pirates, the best guess was that Clemente would be back in Double A ball in a week. He had one foot in the bucket and held his bat at an awkward angle—he looked as though he couldn't hit an outside pitch. A lot of other ballplayers may have had a better-looking stance. Yet they never led the National League in hitting in four different years, the way Clemente did.

Not every ballplayer is born with the ability to hit a curveball. Nor is exceptional hand-eye coordination the key to heavy hitting. Big-league locker rooms are filled with players who have all the attributes, save one: discipline. Every baseball man can tell you a story about a pitcher who throws a ball faster than anyone has ever seen but who has no control on or *off* the field.

The Hall of Fame is full of people who transformed themselves into great ballplayers by working at the sport, by studying the game, and making sacrifices. They're overachievers—and winners. If you want to find them, just watch the World Series. Or simply read about New York Yankee great Lou Gehrig; Ted Williams, "the Splendid Splinter" of the Boston Red Sox; or the Dodgers' strikeout king Sandy Koufax.

A pitcher *should* be able to win a lot of ballgames with a 98-miles-per-hour fastball. But what about the pitcher who wins 20 games a year with a fastball so slow that you can catch it with your teeth? Bob Feller of the Cleveland Indians got into the Hall of Fame with a blazing fastball that glowed in the dark. National League star Grover Cleveland Alexander got there with a pitch that took considerably longer to reach the plate; but when it did arrive, the pitch was exactly where Alexander wanted it to be— and the last place the batter expected it to be.

There are probably more players with exceptional ability who didn't make it to the major leagues than there are who did. A number of great hitters, bored with fielding practice, had to be dropped from their team because their home-run production didn't make up for their lapses in the field. And then there are players like Brooks Robinson of the Baltimore Orioles, who made himself into a human vacuum cleaner at third base because he knew that working hard to become an expert fielder would win him a job in the big leagues.

A star is not something that flashes through the sky. That's a comet. Or a meteor. A star is something you can steer ships by. It stays in place and gives off a steady glow; it is fixed, permanent. A star works at being a star.

And that's how you tell a star in baseball. He shows up night after night and takes pride in how brightly he shines. He's Willie Mays running so hard his hat keeps falling off; Ty Cobb sliding to stretch a single into a double; Lou Gehrig, after being fooled in his first two at-bats, belting the next pitch off the light tower because he's taken the time to study the pitcher. Stars never take themselves for granted. That's why they're stars.

1

THE MIRACLE METS

They were known as the Miracle Mets, and many people believed it. A new expansion team in the National League in 1962, the New York Mets had been a laughable, lovable group of over-the-hill veterans and bumbling beginners that finished either 9th or 10th for each of their first seven years.

Then suddenly, stunningly, unbelievably, these perennial losers, these favorite targets of comedians' jokes, were playing in the 1969 World Series. Not only were the Mets playing in it, but they were leading the heavily favored Baltimore Orioles, two games to one, as their star pitcher, Tom Seaver, finished working on a crossword puzzle and left the clubhouse to warm up for the start of Game 4 at New York's Shea Stadium on October 15.

The Mets had been turned around by a group of young players who were not used to los-ing and had no stake in the team's tradition of clowns. They had a staff of strong-armed young pitchers, including Jerry Koosman, Gary Gentry, Tug McGraw, and a wild, inexperienced Nolan Ryan. Their ace was the handsome, moon-faced, all-American boy, Tom Seaver, who had ridden out of California to rescue the Mets from the baseball dungeon. Seaver had won 25

Tom Seaver goes into his windup during Game 4 of the 1969 World Series. Seaver had been beaten by the highly favored Baltimore Orioles in Game 1, but he came back with a 10-inning, 2–1 victory, and the Miracle Mets stunned the baseball world by winning the Series in five games.

and lost 7 during the 1969 season, with a 2.21 ERA, a record that would earn him the Cy Young Award and just about every other man-of-the-year citation.

As he began his 15-minute warm-up, Seaver went over the scouting reports on the Orioles hitters. The heavily favored Baltimore squad, a team without any obvious weaknesses, had won 109 games. The Mets scouts had cautioned their pitchers about what not to throw Baltimore stars Brooks and Frank Robinson, Boog Powell, and Paul Blair. But they never did say what kind of pitches they *should* throw.

It was cool in the shade of the bullpen. Seaver noticed that the infield was bright with sunshine; he would be moving from a cooler to a warmer place when he went out to throw the first pitch, so there was no need to overdo his warm-up routine. He already felt loose, with perfect timing and rhythm. But he knew that this feeling could be misleading. When he had warmed up before the opening game of the League Championship Series against the Atlanta Braves, he had felt fine. Then he had been belted for 5 runs, even though the Mets pulled out a 9–5 victory.

Seaver had pitched poorly in the Series opener in Baltimore, too. Leading off for the Orioles, Don Buford, his former teammate at the University of Southern California (USC), had hit Seaver's second pitch for a home run. The Mets, stifled by Baltimore right-hander Mike Cuellar, lost the opener, 4–1. But Koosman and Gentry had won the next two games.

As he always did, Seaver looked for his wife, Nancy, in the stands before his first pitch. His whole family was there with her: his mother, father, brother, and two sisters. Then, Don

Buford stepped in to lead off for the Orioles. Seaver's first pitch eased his nervousness, and this time he struck out Buford.

In the second inning, Mets first baseman Donn Clendenon hit a solo home run, and Seaver nursed that 1–0 lead into the ninth.

"We were a little anxious to show the world what we could do," explained Baltimore manager Earl Weaver. "But Seaver was putting them on the corners all day. Even if he fell behind in the count, two balls and no strikes, he still put them on the corners, and our guys were so anxious, they were reaching out and hitting ground balls to the infield."

With one out in the ninth, Frank Robinson and Boog Powell smacked base hits. When Brooks Robinson smoked a line drive into the gap in right center, right fielder Ron Swoboda took off in pursuit and never gave up. With a desperate dive he snagged the ball inches from the grass, but Robinson tagged up and scored the tying run.

Seaver and ace left-hander Jerry Koosman celebrate the Mets' first-ever division title, which the team nailed down with a win over the St. Louis Cardinals on September 24, 1969. Until that moment, the July 20 moon landing by U.S. astronauts had been the event of the year—but for New York baseball fans, nothing could match the triumph of the once-lowly Mets.

In the 10th, the Orioles got two men on base with one out, and Mets pitching coach Rube Walker came out to the mound. "How you feeling?" he asked Seaver, who had learned to be honest and not try to fool himself or his coaches with phony bravado. "I'm tired," Seaver admitted. "But I've got a few pitches left in me."

He stayed in the game, got Buford on a fly ball, and struck out Paul Blair. Win or lose, he had gone as far as he could go. It proved to be enough. In the bottom of the 10th, Mets catcher Jerry Grote wound up on second base when Buford lost his fly ball in the sun. Rod Gaspar ran for Grote. J. C. Martin pinch-hit for Seaver and laid down a sacrifice bunt. Baltimore reliever Pete Richert fielded the bunt and threw to first, but the ball hit Martin on the wrist and caromed away as Gaspar rounded third and tore for home. When his spikes hit the plate, Seaver whooped and hollered as he and the other Mets mobbed the man who had scored the winning run.

Seaver hardly had time to celebrate his first World Series win with his teammates. No sooner did he reach the clubhouse than a Mets official pulled him and Swoboda into a golf cart, which carried them to a room filled with television cameras, microphones, and a crush of reporters. The players answered the same old questions for about an hour, and when they returned to the clubhouse, another swarm of reporters waited with more questions. It was hours after the winning run had been scored before Seaver could relax with the players who remained.

Seaver's family had been waiting patiently, and the happy group went off to a Chinese restaurant, where they talked and sang old

Orioles reliever Pete Richert attempts to throw out New York's J. C. Martin in Game 4 of the 1969 World Series. When the ball hit Martin and bounced away, the winning run scored from second base. The Orioles argued that Martin should have been called out for running inside the base-line, but the umpires let the play star 1, moving the Mets one s' _p closer to a world championship.

songs. Texas native Nolan Ryan, sitting nearby, requested "Home on the Range," and the Seavers gleefully serenaded him.

The next day Jerry Koosman wrapped it up, 5–3, and the Miracle Mets were world champions. In the exuberance that followed, Seaver, the clubhouse cutup, poured champagne over the heads of the chairman of the Mets and the mayor of New York.

Nolan Ryan later said, "There is nothing in sports—no records, no trophies, no amount of money—that can equal the ecstasy of being in a championship clubhouse."

And Tom Seaver realized that no matter how many victories or awards might follow, winning that first World Series, especially when nobody had expected the Mets to be in it, could never be matched. He also knew how much hard work and determination it had taken for him to come this far from the days when he had been "a little shrimp" in Fresno, California, who could not even make a Little League team.

2

THE SHRIMP GROWS UP

Geroge Thomas Seaver was born on November 17, 1944, in Fresno, a city of about 100,000 people in central California. He was named for his grandfather, but from the start his family called him Tom.

Tom was the youngest of four children in a very sports-minded family. His parents were excellent golfers. His sister Katie and brother, Charles, were swimmers at Stanford University. The Seaver children all played golf, tennis, and volleyball and were very competitive. "You get out of something only what you put into it," their father often told them.

Although Tom took an early interest in music and later regretted that he had not taken piano lessons, almost all his time was spent playing whatever sport was in season. Fresno, a fertile fruit- and nut-growing center, has a mild climate all through the year. So Tom was always outdoors.

When he was five, Tom had a friend, Russ Scheidt, who lived across the street on Arthur Avenue. Neither youngster was allowed to cross the busy street, so they sat on opposite curbs and played catch. When Russ was not around, Tom played games in his own yard among the grape and berry vines and the cherry, orange,

Charley Seaver, Tom's father, competes in the 1934 Los Angeles Open. A leading amateur golfer as well as a basketball and football star, the elder Seaver passed on both his athletic ability and his competitive drive to his four children. "You get out of something only what you put into it," he often told them.

15

nectarine, fig, and lemon trees. He created imaginary baseball teams and played out the games on his own, even arguing with the invisible umpires.

His father always urged Tom to believe that he could do whatever he wanted to do, but at the age of eight, Tom learned that this was not necessarily so. One Saturday morning, the North Rotary team in the Fresno Spartan League held tryouts for players nine years old and up. Tom thought he could play well enough to fool the manager, but he was soon found out and sent packing. Deeply disappointed, Tom ran all the way home and cried bitterly. Fortunately, he was not discouraged for long and kept on trying. The next year he made the Little League team as a catcher and infielder.

Fresno is about 300 miles from both San Francisco and Los Angeles, so Tom did not get to see many big league games in person. When he did, he watched the game intently, studying how the big leaguers warmed up, swung the bat, and played their positions. His first major league hero was Hank Aaron, whom he saw on TV hitting three home runs for the Milwaukee Braves in the 1957 World Series. Aaron's consistency and dedication fascinated the youngster.

In high school, Tom did just enough studying to get by; Aaron's batting average and home run totals seemed more important than world history. But as he was playing Babe Ruth League ball, he realized that he was not improving as a hitter, so he began to concentrate on pitching. Looking for a new big leaguer to copy, he chose Sandy Koufax, the Los Angeles Dodgers lefty strikeout king. Again, it was Koufax's consistency and professionalism that Tom most admired.

Tom played basketball at Fresno High to strengthen his legs for pitching, and he was good enough to make the all-city team. But when he was 16 and a junior, he was jolted by the realization that all the other kids had grown in the past few years and he had not.

Tom was a puny 5 feet 8 and weighed barely 145 pounds. His fastball was still a Little League fastball, and for that reason he failed to make the varsity team. With his dream of being a big league pitcher fading, Tom settled for a place on the junior varsity staff. And he was not even the star of the JV team.

But Tom's apparent physical limitations proved to be his key to success. Unlike young athletes who discover the talent and ability that they have, Tom discovered the talent and ability that he did not have. Aware of what he lacked, he concentrated on using his head. He learned that hitters jumped on pitchers' mistakes, so he became determined not to make mistakes. Unable to blow the ball by hitters for strikeouts, he vowed not to give them any free passes to first base. He worked on perfecting the mechanics of his delivery to achieve consistency in throwing every pitch precisely where he wanted it to go.

In his senior year, Tom made the varsity team and was named all-city despite a mediocre 6-5 record. Big league scouts swarmed around the school's star power pitchers with bonus offers, but they ignored Tom. Their eyes popped over a good fastball; anybody could learn control, they said.

When Tom graduated from Fresno High in June 1962, he did not know what he wanted to do next. His brother and two sisters had all gone to college, and his father expected Tom to do the same. But Tom was not ready for college. He stayed home, pitched in the American Legion program, and worked at the raisin-packing plant where his father was a foreman. The raisins were picked and loaded into huge boxes in the fields and brought to the packing plant. They were too heavy for one person to lift, so Tom and another man emptied them, stacked them, and washed them. Sometimes they found a tangle of snakes curled up in a box, and sometimes rats scurried out.

At that time, military service was compulsory, and Tom's father suggested that he fulfill his obligation by joining the Marine Corps Reserve. Tom decided that anything would be better than heaving raisin crates inhabited by snakes and rats. But he soon learned otherwise.

"I hated the Marine Corps boot camp," he wrote later. "Once, I got caught with a dirty rifle, and for three and a half hours I had to do an exercise called up-and-on shoulders, first holding out my rifle, which weighed 11 pounds, then lifting it over my head, then holding it out again. . . . I thought I was going to die. By the end, I couldn't lift my arms."

Tom's boyhood pal Russ Scheidt had joined the Marine Corps with him. One day during dinner, Tom broke the rules by whispering something to Russ. A drill instructor heard him, jumped up on the table, and ran toward Seaver, kicking trays of food every which way and screaming at Tom. As he stood over Tom and chewed him out, the drill instructor kicked him repeatedly in the side.

But at the end of his six months' training, Tom discovered that the Marines had built up his physique. He now stood 6 feet 1 and weighed 195 pounds. And he knew what he wanted to do: go to USC and become a dentist.

Tom was determined to pay for his own education and not rely on his father. So he went to junior college in Fresno, where the tuition was minimal and he could live at home. Besides, Fresno City College had a good baseball team. Aided by the strength he had gained in the Marines, Tom hoped he could pitch well enough to earn a baseball scholarship to USC.

With his newfound fastball, Tom won 11 and lost 2 at Fresno. He attracted some mild attention from scouts and turned down a $2,000 offer to sign with the Dodgers. The USC coach, Rod Dedeaux, showed some interest in Tom, but before offering him a scholarship, Dedeaux asked Tom to go to Alaska to play ball in a semi-pro league.

In the summer of 1964, Tom flew to Fairbanks, Alaska, to pitch for a team known as the Goldpanners. He could not imagine playing baseball in frigid Alaska, and when he got off the plane he was surprised to find the temperature a balmy 75 degrees.

The other players in the league were mostly college students. They had daytime jobs and played ball at night. Tom was also given a job, joining the crew that worked on the playing field. There was plenty of time for baseball after work, because it never gets dark in Fairbanks in the summertime. The sun goes down to the horizon, moves sideways, then rises again. Midnight Sun games began at 11:00 at night, with no lights needed.

In August, the Goldpanners went to the national semipro tournament in Wichita, Kansas. Tom hit a grand slam in one game, but he started and lost the title game. Despite that final disappointment, he had enjoyed the summer. More important, he had pitched well enough to earn the scholarship to USC.

A baby-faced Tom Seaver in the uniform of the Fresno City College Rams. In 1963, fresh out of the Marine Corps, Seaver chalked up an 11–2 record at Fresno and earned a coveted baseball scholarship to the University of Southern California (USC).

3

TOM TERRIFIC

Once he was enrolled at USC, Tom Seaver soon gave up his plans to become a dentist. He studied baseball more than his academic subjects, although English and journalism courses also interested him. He went to Dodgers games and studied the players, lifted weights to build up his shoulder muscles, and practiced different grips that enabled him to make his fastball rise or sink three different ways. Coach Dedeaux impressed on him the value of using his head to outthink each hitter.

Seaver won 10 games in the short college season and returned to Alaska for another summer, working in a sporting goods store by day and pitching by the light of the midnight sun. In the semipro tournament in Wichita, former big leaguers who hit against him told Seaver he had a future as a big league pitcher, and the thought began to occupy his mind.

Baseball was not Seaver's only distraction at USC. At Fresno City College he had noticed a girl named Nancy Lynn McIntyre in one of his classes, but he never spoke to her. On the last day of exams, he spotted her as he was driving away from the school. He stopped his car, ran over, and almost tackled her.

Seaver heads for the USC campus in November 1967 as his wife, Nancy, waves good-bye. Although Seaver had just been named National League Rookie of the Year and had a limitless future in baseball, he was determined to complete his college degree during the off-season.

"Want to go to a softball game?" he asked. The answer was a definite no, but Tom got Nancy into the car and took her to the game anyhow. Nancy was not a baseball fan, but a romance grew from that abrupt beginning, and she and Tom became engaged while he was at USC.

Seaver's reputation as a prospect had also grown. In the major league draft in January 1966, the Atlanta Braves selected him. On February 24, as USC was launching its exhibition season, a Braves scout arrived in Fresno and signed Seaver to a contract that paid him $51,500 in bonuses and incentives.

When the USC coach heard about the signing, he immediately protested, citing a rule that forbade teams from signing college players after their school's playing season had begun. The Braves argued that USC's regular season had not begun, but baseball commissioner William Eckert ruled against them and canceled the contract.

When Seaver went out to pitch for USC, however, the National Collegiate Athletic Association (NCAA), which regulates college sports, declared him ineligible because he had signed a professional contract. It did not matter to the NCAA that Seaver had received no money and the contract had been torn up. As a result, Seaver found himself in a double bind—he could not sign with a major league team, and he could not pitch for USC.

Stung by the unfairness of the situation, Seaver telephoned the commissioner and pleaded his case. Eckert agreed that Seaver's situation was unfair and decided that any team except the Braves could sign Seaver if they matched the Atlanta offer. Three teams—the

Cleveland Indians, Philadelphia Phillies, and New York Mets—offered to match the original terms. On April 2, 1966, the names of the three teams were placed in a hat in the commissioner's office in New York. While Seaver waited on the telephone in Fresno, Eckert drew one name from the hat, and Seaver heard him say, "The winner is . . . the New York Mets."

Two days later, Seaver reported to the Mets minor league training camp in Florida, where he was assigned to the Jacksonville Suns of the AAA International League. However, he met a cool reception from many of the Jacksonville players. Some resented a college boy who had received what was then considered big money just for signing a contract. Others were older players fighting to hold on to their jobs, and they saw every hotshot rookie as a threat. But Seaver made one friend, a rookie shortstop named Bud

If not for USC baseball coach Rod Dedeaux, shown here displaying his 1963 Coach of the Year Award, Seaver might have come to the big leagues as a member of the Atlanta Braves. After Dedeaux protested the Braves' signing of his star pitcher, the commissioner of baseball voided the contract and opened the way for Seaver to sign with the New York Mets.

Harrelson, and they roomed together on the road that year and many years thereafter.

On Monday night, April 25, 1966, Seaver made his professional debut against Rochester, managed by Earl Weaver. Weaver has never forgotten it. "We heard this college pitcher was going to pitch against us and I thought we were going to have an easy night. He beat us, 4 to 2. His slider was low outside, his fastball was up and in; he never missed a corner all night, never threw a ball down the center of the plate all night long. I got on the phone to the Orioles farm director and said, 'I've just seen a guy who's going to the Hall of Fame pitch one ball game, and nobody can be this good. If you ever get a chance to get him, do it.' "

In his next start, Seaver shut out a veteran Buffalo team on two hits. He won his first three games, giving up a total of 12 hits and striking out 27. But he was not happy. He was living in a hotel, and he missed Nancy. He lost his next five games and felt like quitting. Finally, he called Nancy and asked her to come to Florida. She agreed, and the couple were married on June 9.

During the year, Suns manager Solly Hemus had given his rookie pitcher this advice: "Keep a record of everything you do here—how many wind sprints you run, how much sleep you get, what you eat—and see how those things affect your pitching." For the rest of his career, Seaver kept track of all the factors that affected his work. He also noted every pitch he threw and what each hitter did with it. These work habits made him stand out when he arrived at the Mets spring-training camp in 1967.

Catcher Jerry Grote recalled, "The thing that surprised me the most was that whenever I went to the mound, he was never surprised at anything I said. As a rookie, he had a better idea about pitching than 90 percent of the pitchers already in the major leagues."

When the Mets arrived at Shea Stadium to open the season, Seaver found a uniform in his locker with the number 41 on it. Manager Wes Westrum handed Seaver the ball for the second game of the season, on April 13, against the Pittsburgh Pirates. It was a cold day; only 5,005 paying customers saw Seaver's first big league start.

Before the game, Seaver felt sick to his stomach, and his head ached. Unable to summon his usual control, Seaver threw a lot of pitches in the first five innings, allowing two runs, walking six, and striking out eight. With one out in the sixth, Westrum came out to the mound; when Seaver admitted that he was tired, Westrum pulled him, and he ended up with a no-decision.

A week later, Seaver earned his first big league victory, beating the Chicago Cubs, 6–1.

The Mets, who would finish last again in 1967, losing 101 games, were still considered a joke, even by their own fans. Whenever the team won a game, the media made a big deal of it. But Seaver was not part of that tradition of ineptness, and he refused to become part of it. His dedication to excellence extended to all facets of the game: he quickly emerged as an agile, sure-handed fielder and a better-than-average hitter. He also became a loud and lively presence in the clubhouse, teasing his teammates and playing practical jokes.

Reporters covering the team quickly recognized that Seaver's attitude and talent pointed to a new beginning for the Mets. Before long, the

Charley Seaver visits with his son at New York's Shea Stadium in May 1967. The Mets rookie won 16 games in 1967 and posted a sparkling 2.76 ERA; even more important, he established a winning attitude that propelled his team from last place to a world championship in only two years.

papers were calling him Tom Terrific and the Franchise. The players called him Supe or Spanky, because he resembled the leader of the kids in the "Our Gang" comedies.

"I got to see a side of him that most fans never saw," Bud Harrelson recalled. "One time he had really been lit up, and we're in the hotel elevator with a bunch of strangers after the game. He turns to me and says, 'Did Seaver stink out the place tonight or what?' And then he cracked up."

Seaver's biggest thrill as a rookie came when he was named to the 1967 National League All-Star Team. Just 18 months earlier he had been a student at USC, and here he was, in the clubhouse at California's Anaheim Stadium with all the stars he had always thought of as superhuman beings.

"I felt out of place," he recalled, "as if I should still be in the stands wondering what these men are really like." He also looked out of place: Lou Brock thought that he was a batboy and asked him to fetch a soda. But he had a chance to talk to Sandy Koufax, Don Drysdale, Bob Gibson, and other future Hall of Famers he had admired from afar.

Seaver watched the game from the bullpen, not expecting to pitch. But the contest went into extra innings, and when the Nationals took a 2–1 lead in the top of the 15th, manager Walter Alston waved him in to hold the lead. Nervously he strode in from the bullpen. As he passed Roberto Clemente in right field, Seaver said, "Let's get three and go home."

"Go get 'em, kid," Clemente replied.

Seaver then passed Pete Rose at second base. "How about you pitching and me playing second base?" he asked.

Rose laughed. "I'll stay where I am. You can do it."

The chatting helped Seaver relax, but he got goose bumps when he stood on the mound and surveyed his outfield of Clemente, Willie Mays, and Hank Aaron. "What a team of stars behind me and what a thrill," he later wrote. "I'll never forget it." After he struck out the last batter to save the win, Seaver felt a large hand slap him on the back. It was his boyhood idol Henry Aaron.

Seaver finished the 1967 season with a 16-13 record and a 2.76 ERA, winning Rookie of the Year honors. No other Mets pitcher won more than nine games. Tom Terrific had definitely arrived.

4

WINNING IT ALL

O n a spring evening in 1969, four young men stood on a pier in St. Petersburg, Florida, fishing and talking baseball. Tom Seaver, Bud Harrelson, Nolan Ryan, and Jerry Grote were a close foursome. They ate, talked, played cards, and pulled pranks together. None had been in the big leagues more than three years. None was used to playing on losing teams before coming to the Mets.

They talked about the new alignment of the two major leagues, now split into eastern and western divisions. While the media joked that the Mets could not finish ninth again because there were only six teams in their division, the thoughtful players analyzed the competition and concluded that the Mets might be good enough to finish first: they had a nucleus of talented young players, and in 1968 they had acquired a first-rate manager in Gil Hodges. Following each day's spring-training workouts, the four budding Mets stars pumped up their confidence. But they said nothing publicly about their hopes; this was not the kind of talk that anyone would seriously link with the New York Mets.

In St. Petersburg, pitching coach Rube Walker helped Seaver develop a better curve to go with his improving fastball and slider. As he

Seaver and Mets manager Gil Hodges pose for photographers before the opening of the 1969 National League playoffs. Seaver's 1969 performance— 25 wins and a 2.21 ERA—established him as baseball's best pitcher; he gave much of the credit for his success to Hodges, who, he said, "taught me how to be a pro."

matured, Seaver became more of a "leg" pitcher. A pitcher's power comes from the legs and buttocks, and when Seaver reached his ideal playing weight of 205, much of it was added to those areas. Nolan Ryan and Roger Clemens became similar leg pitchers.

Seaver also perfected his mechanics: the step forward with the left foot always landing in the same spot, the right arm wheeling over his shoulder. His powerful follow-through caused his right knee and foot to scrape the surface of the mound, forcing him to wear padding across the top of his shoe. A big dirt stain on his right knee became a sure sign that Seaver was on his game.

Seaver felt ready for a big year in 1969, but the team looked like the same old Mets when they gave away two runs in the first inning and lost the opener, 11–10, to the Montreal Expos, the National League's latest expansion team. Seaver lasted only five innings.

The big guns of the Mets pitching staff—Seaver, Jerry Koosman, Gary Gentry, and Nolan Ryan— pause during a workout at Shea Stadium in 1969. At the start of the season, Gil Hodges had cautiously predicted 85 victories for his team; relying on superb pitching and tight defense, the Mets astonished the sports world by winning 100 games.

During the first weeks of the season, the Mets lost more often than they won. Then they perked up and on May 21 raised their record to 18-18 when Seaver blanked Atlanta, 5–0. It was the first time in the Mets' eight-year history that they had reached the .500 mark. This miraculous event inspired a celebration in the clubhouse that left Seaver and his friends dumbstruck. When a grinning reporter asked him what he thought of the joyous occasion, Seaver glared at him. "We haven't done anything yet," he muttered.

The .500-level balloon promptly burst as the Mets lost their next five games. But they suddenly won 11 straight; on the morning of July 9, they found themselves in the unfamiliar neighborhood of second place, five games behind the Chicago Cubs, as Seaver faced the league leaders before a record crowd at Shea Stadium.

Everything worked for Seaver that night: rising and sinking fastballs, fast and slow curves, sharp sliders. He was in a groove where every pitch went exactly where he intended it to go. For eight innings, not a single Cub reached first base. When Seaver took the mound in the ninth, leading 4–0, he was well aware that he was just three outs from a perfect game, something only eight pitchers in the history of baseball had accomplished. His heart was beating so hard that he lost the feeling in his right arm. But he kept telling himself, "I can do it."

The first batter laid down a bunt, but Seaver, always an excellent fielder, reached the ball in plenty of time. One out. Then Jimmy Qualls, a light-hitting rookie who was to accumulate only 31 base hits in a brief big league career, got a sinker that failed to sink and lined it to left center for a clean single.

"It was just like everything ran out through the bottom of my feet," Seaver said later. "Never in any aspect of my life had I experienced such a disappointment." He always considered that game the best he ever pitched, and once the pain subsided he began referring to it wryly as "my imperfect game."

With a 14-3 record at midseason, Seaver developed stiffness in his right shoulder and lost four of his next five starts. At the All-Star break, the Mets were still close on the heels of the Cubs, but the experts expected them to fade like last summer's suntan. By mid-August it looked as if the pundits were right; the Mets fell to third place, 9½ games out. Even Seaver began to look ahead to next year.

But all at once the Mets started winning, and the Cubs began to stumble. When the Mets took a series from the Dodgers with a 1–0, 15-inning victory, Seaver remembered "going into the club-house and making eye contact with Grote. It was like an electrical charge."

Down the stretch, Seaver won 10 in a row to finish with a 25-7 record, but for the surging Mets every day saw a different hero driving in the winning run or making the sensational game-saving catch. Relief pitcher Tug McGraw worked his way out of every jam he waded into.

Manager Gil Hodges had spent his first year studying his players until he knew them inside and out. One of the strongest men ever to play the game, Hodges had been a slugging first baseman on the great Brooklyn Dodgers teams of the 1950s. He tolerated no nonsense and commanded total respect. In 1969, every move he made seemed to work. Always calm and dig-nified, Hodges never panicked or yelled, but he

got his message across. He let every player know what was expected of him and made each man feel that he was contributing toward the goal of winning.

On one occasion, Seaver blew a 5–0 lead against the San Francisco Giants when he tightened up on the mound and lost his rhythm. On his next start, he decided to relax and fool around a little. He won the game but pitched poorly. Afterward, Hodges said to him, "I didn't like what you were doing on the field today." Seaver explained that he had been acting as if he did not care, just to stay loose.

Hodges told him it did not matter if it was hot or cold, what the size of the crowd was, whom

While a capacity crowd watches the Mets win the World Series at Shea Stadium on October 16, 1969, the sign held aloft by a die-hard fan sums up the team's improbable rise from clowns to world champions. When left fielder Cleon Jones snagged Davey Johnson's fly ball for the final out, the fans erupted in a celebration that nearly wrecked the ballpark.

the Mets were playing, or where they stood in the pennant race. "Go about your job in a professional way every day, and know that you can control yourself . . . winning or losing."

Seaver never forgot that lesson. "A pitcher should control his emotions as much as possible," he later wrote. "He shouldn't permit umpires' calls, errors and mental lapses by himself or his teammates to affect him. I try to control my emotions by getting things off my chest. When I get upset, I'll turn to the outfield, and do a lot of swearing. I'm not swearing at anyone in particular, just blowing off steam and only for the moment."

But he did not always succeed. Once in St. Louis he made a bad pitch and came back into the dugout and kicked the water cooler so hard that it broke away from the water pipe. The water gushed out and flooded the dugout. Somebody said, "Hey, the guy didn't hit a home run off you." "That wasn't it," Seaver replied. "I missed with that pitch."

In the last month of the 1969 season, Seaver was almost unhittable, as the Mets went 38-10 down the stretch and clinched the division title on September 24. They did not play especially well in the playoffs against the Atlanta Braves, but they won three straight games and went on to shock the baseball world by capturing the world championship, beating the heavily favored Baltimore Orioles in the World Series.

Seaver's 25 wins, 2.21 ERA, and 208 strikeouts earned him the Cy Young Award, the Hickok Belt as the nation's outstanding professional athlete, and *Sports Illustrated*'s Sportsman of the Year title. He was happy to have the

Seaver and Koosman (who won the deciding game of the Series) revel in the Broadway ticker-tape parade honoring the world champion Mets. During the off-season, Seaver won the N.L. Cy Young Award and finished a close second in the voting for the Most Valuable Player Award, which went to San Francisco Giants slugger Willie McCovey.

honors, but he now realized that the awards and celebrations were secondary and that "the real thrill had been back there in the competition on the field."

5

"YOU GOTTA BELIEVE!"

Life can be hectic for world champions in the months following their victory, especially in New York. During the 1969–70 off-season, Tom Seaver received hundreds of requests to speak at banquets. Books, business deals, television appearances, and product endorsements flowed his way. He took a pie in the face on one TV show. Some enterprising producer wanted him and Nancy to star in a play, but acting was not for them. In the middle of all this activity, Seaver came out of his apartment one morning in December and discovered that his dark brown 1968 Porsche had been stolen: there were some things even a World Series ring could not prevent.

Seaver was happy when it came time to head for Florida and spring training. But this time things were different. The Mets were no longer laughed at; having become winners, they were now expected to win every year. Seaver's salary, now $80,000, had catapulted him to the top echelon in the game: anything less than 25 wins would now be considered disappointing by fans and experts.

But the Mets were out of miracles. They finished either third or fourth for the next three years, although Seaver won 18, 20, and 21.

Seaver in the midst of a 3–0 whitewash of the Philadelphia Phillies on opening day of the 1973 season. Seaver went on to win 19 games during the season, and the Mets caught fire in September, capturing their second division title.

There were some personal highlights for the Mets ace: a National League record 19 strikeouts against the San Diego Padres, including the last 10 batters in a row, on April 22, 1970; twice hitting game-winning home runs; taking a no-hitter into the ninth against San Diego on July 4, 1972; and pitching another one-hitter in 1971.

Going for win number 20 against the Cardinals on the last night of the 1971 season, Seaver was startled late in the game when the crowd began cheering. Then he looked at the scoreboard, which announced that he had just broken the league record for strikeouts in a season by a right-handed pitcher: 289. But the cheers and the records were small consolation as he watched other teams celebrate World Series victories. "It's a sad feeling to watch it on TV from afar and not be a part of it," he said.

The brightest spot for Seaver during this time was the birth of his first daughter, Sarah, on February 24, 1971. And the saddest event occurred just before the 1972 season opened, when Mets manager Gil Hodges suffered a fatal heart attack. "I loved the man," Seaver said, "and I tremendously admired him."

Hampered by injuries, the Mets got off to a stumbling start in 1973 under their new manager, Yogi Berra. They took up residence in last place, but nobody else was playing well, either, so they did not drop out of sight. Seaver's fastball kept getting him into trouble, and he was not winning with it consistently, so he did what he had always been able to do: adjust. He concentrated more on perfecting his other pitches and outthinking the hitters. Dave Winfield, a rookie with San Diego in 1973, recalled what it was like to face Seaver: "Before the game, in the twilight of Shea Stadium, you're sitting in those low dugouts, looking up out at that mound, and he's warming up and the ball is booming into the catcher's mitt and the dust is flying, and the airplanes are buzzing into the airport next door—and you don't need any distraction like that. That's a challenge. That's a tough situation. . . . Seaver taught me a lesson: he was the first pitcher who went up the ladder on me. First pitch—fastball waist high. Strike one. Next pitch—fastball a little higher, across the letters. Strike two. Next pitch—fastball a little higher. I couldn't lay off it. Swing and a miss. Strike three. . . . Seaver is among the top five pitchers I ever faced. You knew every time out, he was going to be good."

Still the Mets struggled. In mid-July they were 12 games out. A month later they were still in last place, but only 7½ back of the first-place Cardinals. After they lost to the Reds on August 17, Mets chairman M. Donald Grant made a rare appearance in the clubhouse. In a short speech, he told the players they had to believe in

Mets reliever Tug McGraw fires his legendary screwball in 1973. With the team mired in last place in the middle of August, McGraw coined his now-famous slogan, "You gotta believe!" His high spirits and brilliant relief pitching were major factors in the Mets pennant drive.

themselves to win. When he finished, reliever Tug McGraw, who had been thinking the same thing on his way to the ballpark, leaped on a chair and began to shout, "You gotta believe! You gotta believe!" The media picked up the slogan, and soon the fans began chanting it and printing it on banners. "You gotta believe!" became the Mets' 1973 battle cry.

When they took four out of five from the Pirates, the Mets actually did begin to believe. With five teams in the race down to the wire, the Mets squeaked through on the last day to win the division title with a modest 82-79 record.

In the West, Cincinnati's Big Red Machine, led by Pete Rose, Johnny Bench, Joe Morgan, and Tony Perez, had won 99 games and rolled to a second straight title. They beat Seaver in the playoff opener, 2–1, on late-inning home runs by Bench and Rose, negating a brilliant performance in which Seaver had relentlessly challenged the hard-hitting Reds with blazing fastballs, striking out 13. In Game 2, the Mets bounced back as lefty Jon Matlack shut out the Reds on two hits. Back at Shea Stadium for Game 3, the Mets were coasting with a 9–2 lead in the top of the fifth inning when a frustrated Rose slid hard into second base, flattening shortstop Bud Harrelson. The two exchanged words, and suddenly Rose and the mild-mannered Harrelson were wrestling atop second base. Both benches emptied, and the ensuing brawl was highlighted by the sight of Cincinnati reliever Pedro Borbon shredding a Mets cap with his teeth.

When the Mets came to bat and Rose took up his position in left field, Mets fans unloaded a barrage of objects at him, including a bottle that

narrowly missed his head. Reds manager Sparky Anderson immediately pulled his team off the field, and the umpires threatened to forfeit the game to the Reds unless the Mets could get the crowd under control. Seaver, Berra, and a few other Mets sprinted out to left field and pleaded with the outraged fans to cool it. The appeal worked, and the Mets nailed down their second victory.

The Reds came back to win Game 4, and the best-of-five-games series headed for a showdown at Shea. Warming up before the final game, Seaver, who had been plagued by shoulder pain for a month, could not get the pop he wanted on his fastball. He relied on breaking balls and change-ups to beat the Reds, 7–2. The Mets were in their second World Series.

The Mets and the defending world champions, the Oakland A's, seesawed through a seven-game Series. Seaver started Game 3 and had a no-decision in an 11-inning, 3–2 Mets loss. He came back in Game 6 and trailed 2–0

Cincinnati's Pete Rose (left) and Mets shortstop Bud Harrelson tangle at second base during the 1973 N.L. playoffs. The incident began with a hard take-out slide by Rose and escalated into a near-riot. When the dust cleared, the Mets wrapped up a 9–2 win over the favored Reds.

With Oakland A's shortstop Bert Campaneris at bat, Seaver delivers the first pitch of Game 3 of the 1973 World Series. Seaver pitched a strong game, striking out 12 before being lifted for a pinch hitter in the eighth inning. The A's ground out an 11-inning, 3–2 victory, en route to their second straight world championship.

when a cold wind stiffened his arm. He left the game after seven innings and took the loss.

This time there was no miracle for New York. The A's, led by Reggie Jackson, Bert Campaneris, and Catfish Hunter, won the seventh game in Oakland and whooped it up while the tired Mets went home. "I was glad I didn't have to pack my bags and get on another airplane and go to another hotel," Seaver said.

Seaver's performance in 1973 earned him his second Cy Young Award and a contract for $172,500, making him at that time the highest-paid pitcher in history. But the following spring, his attempts to favor his sore shoulder led to problems with his hips and back. Never comfortable, he struggled to an 11-11 record and struck out 201, his lowest total in seven years. "At times I got completely lost," he admitted. "The harder I tried, it seemed the deeper I went into the pit."

For the first time, Seaver was booed at Shea Stadium. "They're not booing me," he told a

writer. "They're booing who they think Tom Seaver is. They relate to an image they have of me . . . from articles or short TV interviews. . . . It may not be close to what I am. . . . I want to retain as much of my privacy as I can."

Some people delighted in knocking him, in print or in the ballpark, because they perceived his strong self-confidence as arrogance. But they did not know the Tom Seaver who never pitched a game he did not expect to win; who enjoyed being amid the players, umpires, and fans and facing a hitter one-on-one; who played rock music on the way to the ballpark and symphonies on the way home; who called his wife every night the team was on the road, talked it out after a poor outing, and started afresh the next time; whose roommate, Bud Harrelson, knew it was best to leave him alone after a bad game, and especially not to play country music on the guitar in their hotel room.

Dismayed by the poor job he had done, Seaver took a pay cut for 1975. Although the Mets slipped to third, he came back to lead the league with 22 wins and 243 strikeouts, good enough to win his third Cy Young Award. The only thing that still eluded him was a no-hitter: on September 24 at Chicago, he had again lost his bid to an obscure rookie in the ninth, when Joe "Tarzan" Wallis got a two-out single for the Cubs.

In October, the Seavers' second daughter, Anne, was born. Settled into a comfortable household that included two dogs, Slider and Hot Stuff, and a cat named Fergie, Tom looked forward to many more victories in a New York uniform. The victories were to come, but the uniform was destined to change.

6

MOVING ON

Seaver fights back tears as he talks to reporters on June 16, 1977, following his trade to the Cincinnati Reds. Unable to speak, Seaver finally wrote out a brief statement, expressing his gratitude to the New York fans, and left the ballpark.

On the sunny afternoon of June 15, 1977, Tom Seaver sat beside a swimming pool at an Atlanta hotel and concluded that his days with the Mets were nearing an end. The trouble had begun when he held out in 1976. The Mets had offered him a base salary with bonuses if he achieved certain goals. Seaver wanted a straight salary; he believed he had proven his worth to the team. His lifetime ERA of 2.47 was the best of any pitcher who had worked at least 2,000 innings. Forty percent of the Mets' attendance had come through the turnstiles on the days he pitched.

But the split went deeper than money. Always outspoken, sometimes too much for his own good, Seaver had publicly criticized the Mets management for failing to get the players the team needed in order to win. He was also the team's union representative and played a major role in the players' ongoing battle for free agency and other changes in the system.

When Seaver's feud with the Mets went public, Donald Grant claimed that the holdout destroyed the team's family image. He called Seaver an ingrate and secretly worked on a deal that would send Seaver to the Los Angeles Dodgers. When word of the impending trade got out, Mets fans raised a howl of protest, and Grant canceled the deal. Seaver, expressing his loyalty to the Mets, signed a three-year contract.

The 1976 season was long and dreary. The Mets finished third, and Seaver slipped to 14-11, although he led the league in strikeouts for the fifth and last time. That winter was a happier time for the Seavers. They bought an old barn in Greenwich, Connecticut, complete with haylofts and horse stalls, and began converting it into a house. They had to chase out the bats living in the big fireplaces, but they allowed the deer and pheasants to wander in the yard. Seaver helped design the rooms and finish the floors, and he made a breakfast table from an old barn door.

However, the bickering between Seaver and the Mets continued in the spring of 1977. They accused him of wanting to renegotiate his contract, now that players on other teams were beginning to get million-dollar deals. Seaver said he wanted only an extension of his contract in keeping with the new, higher salary levels. Again, the Mets called him disloyal. In spring training Seaver admitted to reporters, "For the first time, I feel much of the joy is gone. I still have professional pride, but the larger feeling for the club is gone."

The fuss continued into the season, with writers and broadcasters taking one side or the other. As the trading deadline of June 15 neared, Seaver was aware that the Mets were shopping him around. On Sunday, June 12, he pitched a five-hitter for his seventh win against three losses, but he took no real pleasure in it. "It tore my heart out to know that might be the last game I would pitch for the Mets, to think of leaving people like Harrelson and Koosman," he told a reporter.

Finally, as he sat brooding beside the pool on the afternoon of June 15, a reporter sat down beside him and read him a column written by veteran sportswriter Dick Young, who was known to be close to Donald Grant. Young put all the blame for the squabble on Nancy Seaver. She was jealous, he claimed, because the Seavers' friends Nolan and Ruth Ryan now had more money, and she was pushing her husband to make demands on the Mets. (Committing one of the greatest blunders in baseball history, the Mets had traded Ryan to the California Angels in 1972; he quickly emerged as a superstar and was lavishly rewarded by Angels owner Gene Autry.) When he heard what Young had written, Seaver became so furious that he raced to a telephone, called the Mets, and demanded to be traded. Before the day was over, the best pitcher in baseball had been sent to the Cincinnati Reds for four players.

The next day, at a press conference in the Mets clubhouse, Seaver's normal cool deserted him. When asked how he felt about the New York fans, he could not speak. Choking back tears, he asked for a break, walked away for about 10 minutes, then returned.

"As far as the fans go, I've given them a great number of thrills, and they've been equally returned. The ovation I got the other night—" He lowered his head and began to sob. Tapping his heart, he muttered, "Come on, George." But he could not continue. He took a reporter's notebook and said, "I'll have to write it out." As the TV cameras rolled and the press waited, he sat and wrote, then asked a newsman to read: "And the ovation I got the other night after passing Sandy Koufax [in career strikeouts] will be one of the most memorable and warm moments in my life." Then, asking to be excused, he picked up his gear and left.

Sparky Anderson, the easygoing, popular manager of the Cincinnati Reds, was apprehensive about the arrival of Seaver, the big New York star. "But within a week I knew he was a regular guy," Anderson recalled. "He had no swelled head. He was the same with a young guy as with Pete Rose or Johnny Bench. And the young pitchers hung on his shirttails. He has class as a pitcher and a person. And that was the one thing I wanted my players to have more than anything else—class."

In his first game for the Reds, Seaver beat the Expos, 6–0. He went on to win 14 and lose 3 for Cincinnati. Without question, the highlight of the year for Seaver was the night of August 21, when he returned to Shea Stadium and pitched against Jerry Koosman and the Mets. "I kept saying it was not emotional," he admitted later, "but I had to say that to keep it all down inside of me. I'd be lying if I said it was not an emotional game for me." He beat the Mets, 5–1, and every move he made was greeted with an ovation from the hometown fans.

Seaver was far from being the Reds' highest-paid player, but that did not bother him. He was embarrassed and frustrated when he got off to a 1-4 start in 1978. The Reds had a chance to win the pennant, and he was trying to win it all by himself every time he pitched. But he could no longer blow his fastball by the hitters, and he had to rely on control and changing speeds.

Just as slumping hitters are inundated with advice, Seaver got plenty of help. Former teammates Koosman and Ryan told him he was overthrowing. His mother reminded him to slow

down. "She's been doing that for 20 years," he said. "When I was just a little kid pitching, I could hear her in the stands yelling, 'Slow down, slow down.' And she's right."

On June 16, 1978, Seaver finally got past that ninth-inning jinx and pitched a 4–0 no-hitter against the Cardinals. He finished the year with a 16-14 record, and the Reds finished second to the Dodgers in the N.L. West.

Seaver again won 16 games for the Western Division champion Reds in 1979. But the Pirates swept the Reds in the playoff and went to the World Series. Plagued by his first sore arm, Seaver won only 10 games against 8 losses the following year. That winter he worked on his first off-season exercise and throwing program, while a poster of Henry Aaron looked down at him from the garage wall. He was 36, and he still had goals to reach.

Seaver and Hall of Fame catcher Johnny Bench limber up at the Cincinnati Reds spring training camp in Tampa, Florida. Though he was always a Met at heart, Seaver pitched some memorable games in a Cincinnati uniform, including his only no-hitter, a 4–0 victory over the Cardinals on June 16, 1978.

7

BOWING OUT

On April 19, 1981, Tom Seaver reached one of his major goals by chalking up his 3,000th strikeout. Relying on control and brains, he went 14-2 during a season that was shortened by two months because of a players' strike. He would have won an unprecedented fourth Cy Young Award, if not for the emergence of Fernando Valenzuela: the Dodgers rookie southpaw had posted lesser numbers, but his storybook climb from rural poverty in Mexico to big league stardom had captured the imagination of the baseball world.

Cincinnati fell all the way to last place in 1982, and Seaver was part of the problem. Trying to compensate for a pulled muscle and other injuries, he messed up his mechanics and had his worst year—5-13. His earned run average soared to 5.50. Seaver's 111 innings pitched and 62 strikeouts were career lows, and he failed to pitch a single complete game for the only time in his 20-year career.

The Reds looked at Seaver's big salary, advanced age (38), and poor record and decided he was history. They traded him back to the Mets, now under new management, for three minor leaguers. His old uniform with the 41 on it was waiting for him.

Seaver deposits his gear in the Mets locker room once again, following his 1982 trade back to New York. Rebounding from an injury-plagued season, Seaver notched 201 strikeouts in 1983, but he was pitching for a last-place team and struggled to a 9-14 record.

51

When the public address announcer stated the starting lineup for the Mets on opening day at Shea Stadium in 1983, he ended by saying, "Pitching for the Mets, number forty-one." No name was necessary for the 51,000 fans, who erupted in a thunderous ovation. As Seaver walked in from the bullpen after warming up, he noticed a boy on crutches in the stands near the field and handed him the ball he had used warming up. Although he had to leave the game after six innings with a leg injury, he was the pitcher of record in a 2–0 Mets win.

Seaver proved he was not through, working more than 200 innings and fanning 201, his highest totals in five years. But the Mets had no hitting and finished last. Seaver had to work hard to win 9 games while losing 14.

During the off-season, the Mets left Seaver's name off their list of protected players, which meant that another team could claim him if they lost a top player as a free agent. The Mets management said that the only reason for this move was to protect their younger players; they believed that Seaver's age and salary would discourage anyone from claiming him. But some reporters hinted that Seaver's relations with the club's front office were still strained. Whatever the case, the Chicago White Sox put in a claim, and Seaver suddenly found himself working in another midwestern city, far from his Connecticut home.

Seaver felt like a visitor during his two years in Chicago. He and his family lived in a rented apartment each summer and went sightseeing like other tourists. But in the clubhouse and on the field Seaver remained, in manager Tony LaRussa's words, "a complete professional." Tim Hulett, an infielder with the Sox, recalled, "He

was the most easily recognized player on the team and was always swarmed around by fans wherever we went. But he always was courteous to everybody. He was quiet in the clubhouse, sitting there working crossword puzzles, but he would help anyone who asked him."

The White Sox were going nowhere, but Seaver worked toward fulfilling his goals. He went 15-11 and 16-11, worked 238 innings at the age of 40, and struck out 134 in 1985, his second-highest total in eight years. His 3.17 ERA was his best in four years. But his biggest win came on August 4, 1985, in New York, this time at Yankee Stadium. Going into the game his victory total stood at 299, and this was his first try for 300. At 5:30 that morning he and Nancy had been awakened by a bat fluttering about in their bedroom. They chased it with a broom, but there was to be no more sleep for Seaver on the day when he would try to become the 17th pitcher ever to reach 300 wins.

As he got into his uniform in the clubhouse, the equipment man handed him a ball and said that the Yankees' Rickey Henderson had sent it over and asked him to sign it. It reminded Seaver

On the road again in 1984, Seaver toils for the Chicago White Sox. Though his big fastball was only a memory, Seaver still knew how to get hitters out. He won 31 games during his two years with the Chisox and became only the 17th pitcher in major league history to post 300 victories.

that 18 years earlier he had gone into the Milwaukee Braves clubhouse and asked Henry Aaron for his autograph.

Warming up during a pregame ceremony that honored Yankees favorite Phil Rizzuto, Seaver's stomach hurt and his head ached. He felt as rotten as he had before his first big league start. His father and father-in-law, along with Nancy, Sarah, and Annie, were among the 54,000 spectators in Yankee Stadium. Seaver soon realized that his daughters were less than awed by the occasion.

Leading 4–1 in the eighth, Seaver struck out Dave Winfield with two on and two out. While putting on his jacket beside the dugout, he said to nine-year-old Annie, "Just three more outs." "Good," she replied, "then we can go home and go swimming." The Yankees got two men on base with two out in the ninth, but Don Baylor flied out to left, and Tom Seaver had reached the second of his career goals.

Soon after pitching a record 16th opening day game in 1986, Seaver was traded to the Boston Red Sox. He was happy to be closer to home, although he really wanted to finish his career in New York. His last win, number 311, was on August 17, 1986, over the Twins in Minnesota. He was 5-7 for the pennant-winning Red Sox, but a knee injury suffered in his last game on September 19 kept him from pitching against the Mets in the World Series.

Released by the Red Sox at the end of the year and having passed Walter Johnson on the all-time strikeout list, Tom Seaver, now 42, was not interested in pitching anywhere that would take him far from home. The Yankees invited him to spring training, but they offered no contract. When the Mets ran short of healthy pitch-

Taking the mound for one last time at Shea, Seaver expresses his thanks to the New York fans during the Tom Seaver Day festivities July 24, 1988. Following the ceremonies, Seaver's number 41 was enshrined on the outfield wall, joining the numbers of two other immortal Mets, former managers Casey Stengel (37) and Gil Hodges (14).

ers, they asked their former ace to work out at Shea Stadium. But Seaver's shoulder ached, and he pitched poorly against a farm team; he knew his playing days were over. On June 22, 1987, in the Mets clubhouse, he announced his retirement.

A year later, the Mets retired his number 41, which Seaver considered a bigger thrill than being inducted into the Hall of Fame. On July 24, 1988, he told a crowd of 46,057 at Shea Stadium, "I came to a decision a long time ago, if my number was retired, there was one way I wanted to say thank you. If you will allow me one moment, I want to say thank you in a very special way. If you know me and how much I love pitching, you'll know what this means to me." Dressed in a business suit, with no glove or ball, he jogged out to the mound and stood on the rubber. Facing the right field foul pole, he began turning slowly, bowing and blowing kisses to the crowd, until he worked his way all around the field. Then he joined his wife and daughters in a convertible the Mets had given him and drove off through the center-field gate.

Seaver was interested in becoming a manager or general manager, but when no offers came, he joined the Yankees broadcasting crew. Then, on the evening of January 8, 1992, Seaver learned that he had been elected to the Baseball Hall of Fame with a 98.8 percent vote, the highest to date. Seaver first expressed amazement at the vote, then said, "There are moments in an individual's life that he will take with him forever. This is one. . . . I don't suppose this is really going to hit me until I walk the halls at Cooperstown next August to look at the plaque of Christy Mathewson. My children will be able to take their children to the Hall of Fame and say, 'There's your grandfather. In his day he was pretty good.' It's a wonderful thing to think about."

Baseball Commissioner Fay Vincent joins Seaver and former Oakland A's reliever Rollie Fingers at a 1992 news conference announcing the election of the two great hurlers to the Hall of Fame. Seaver's 98.8 percent vote was the highest in the history of Hall of Fame balloting.

One of the first calls Seaver made after hearing the news was to Russ Scheidt, who had played catch with him across the street when they were children in Fresno. He invited Scheidt to come to the Hall of Fame induction ceremony as his guest. In his induction speech, Seaver paid tribute to Gil Hodges, "who taught me how to really be a pro." He spoke of the infielders who contribute so much to any pitcher's winning record but seldom get the praise they deserve. He closed by calling the day "the last beautiful flower in a perfect bouquet."

Tom Seaver always expressed confidence in his own abilities. In 1982 he had listed for a group of Boy Scouts his keys to staying on top of life's game: "Concentration, hard work and dedication. No one can lift the weights, do the sit-ups or any of the other work for you. I know it sounds egotistical, but Mets manager Gil Hodges didn't make me. Neither did my father or pitching coach Rube Walker. I am the person most responsible for my success."

The veteran pitcher and manager Roger Craig once said, "A pitcher gets to the major leagues on ability; he becomes great because of mental toughness."

That was Tom Terrific to a T.

CHRONOLOGY

1944	Born in Fresno, California, on November 17
1962	Graduates from Fresno High School; joins Marine Corps Reserve
1963	Enrolls at Fresno Community College, compiling 11-2 record as a pitcher
1964	Plays semipro ball for Fairbanks Goldpanners in Alaska; wins scholarship to the University of Southern California (USC)
1966	Signs with Atlanta Braves; contract voided by commissioner; signs with New York Mets; marries Nancy McIntyre on June 9
1967	Makes major league debut on April 13; earns first major league win on April 20; appears in first All-Star Game on July 11; named N.L. Rookie of the Year
1969	Wins 25 games and leads Mets to world championship; wins first of three Cy Young Awards
1971	Daughter Sarah is born on February 24
1973	Wins second Cy Young Award as Mets capture their second N.L. pennant
1974	Becomes highest-paid pitcher in baseball history; completes B.A. degree in public relations at USC
1975	Wins third Cy Young Award; daughter Anne is born on October 28
1977	Traded to Cincinnati Reds on June 15
1978	Pitches no-hitter vs. St. Louis Cardinals on June 16
1981	Records 3,000th strikeout on September 18
1982	Traded back to New York Mets on December 16
1984	Claimed by Chicago White Sox in free agent compensation pool on January 20
1985	Wins 300th game on August 4
1986	Traded to Boston Red Sox on June 29; wins 311th and final game on August 15
1987	Announces retirement on June 22
1992	Elected to National Baseball Hall of Fame with record 98.8 percent vote

GEORGE THOMAS SEAVER

NEW YORK, N.L., 1967-1977, 1983
CINCINNATI, N.L., 1977-1982
CHICAGO, A.L., 1984-1986
BOSTON, A.L., 1986

FRANCHISE POWER PITCHER WHO TRANSFORMED
METS FROM LOVABLE LOSERS INTO FORMIDABLE
FOES. WON 311 GAMES OVER 20 SEASONS. SET N.L.
CAREER RECORD FOR STRIKEOUTS BY RHP (3,272)
AND MODERN RECORD FOR LOWEST ERA (2.73).
WHIFFED 200 OR MORE N.L. RECORD 10 TIMES
(19 IN A SINGLE GAME). N.L. ROOKIE OF YEAR,
1967 AND 3-TIME CY YOUNG AWARDEE. NO-HIT
CARDS IN 1978.

MAJOR LEAGUE STATISTICS

NEW YORK METS, CINCINNATI REDS, CHICAGO WHITE SOX, BOSTON RED SOX

YEAR	TEAM	W	L	PCT	ERA	G	GS	CG	IP	H	BB	SO	ShO
1967	NY N	16	13	.552	2.76	35	34	18	251	224	78	170	2
1968		16	12	.571	2.20	36	35	14	278	224	48	205	5
1969		25	7	.781	2.21	36	35	18	273.1	202	82	208	5
1970		18	12	.600	2.81	37	36	19	291	230	83	283	2
1971		20	10	.667	1.76	36	35	21	286	210	61	289	4
1972		21	12	.636	2.92	35	35	13	262	215	77	249	3
1973		19	10	.655	2.08	36	36	18	290	219	64	251	3
1974		11	11	.500	3.20	32	32	12	236	199	75	201	5
1975		22	9	.710	2.38	36	36	15	280	217	88	243	5
1976		14	11	.560	2.59	35	34	13	271	211	77	235	5
1977	2 teams	NY N (13G 7–3)		CIN N (20G 14–3)									
"	total	21	6	.778	2.58	33	33	19	261.1	199	66	196	7
1978	CIN N	16	14	.533	2.87	36	36	8	260	218	89	226	1
1979		16	6	.727	3.14	32	32	9	215	187	61	131	5
1980		10	8	.556	3.64	26	26	5	168	140	59	101	1
1981		14	2	.875	2.55	23	23	6	166	120	66	87	1
1982		5	13	.278	5.50	21	21	0	111.1	136	44	62	0
1983	NY N	9	14	.391	3.55	34	34	5	231	201	86	135	2
1984	CHI A	15	11	.577	3.95	34	33	10	236.2	216	61	131	4
1985		16	11	.593	3.17	35	33	6	238.2	223	69	134	1
1986	2 teams	CHI A (12G 2–6)		BOS A (16G 5–7)									
"	total	7	13	.350	4.03	28	28	2	176.1	180	56	103	0
Totals		311	205	.603	2.86	656	647	231	4782.2	3971	1390	3640	61

World Series

YEAR	TEAM	W	L	PCT	ERA	G	GS	CG	IP	H	BB	SO	ShO
1969	NY N	1	1	.500	3.00	2	2	1	15	12	3	9	0
1973		0	1	.000	2.40	2	2	0	15	13	3	18	0
Totals		1	2	.333	2.70	4	4	1	30	25	6	27	0

FURTHER READING

Breslin, Jimmy. *Can't Anybody Here Play This Game?* New York: Penguin, 1982.

Cohen, Joel H. *Inside Corner: Talks with Tom Seaver.* New York: Atheneum, 1974.

Cohen, Stanley. *A Magic Summer: The '69 Mets.* San Diego, CA: Harcourt Brace Jovanovich, 1988.

Felser, Larry. *Baseball's 10 Greatest Players.* New York: Scholastic, 1979.

Honig, Donald. *The New York Mets: The First Quarter Century.* New York: Crown, 1986.

Ryan, Nolan, with Mickey Herskowitz. *Kings of the Hill.* New York: HarperCollins, 1992.

Seaver, Tom, and Dick Belsky. *Baseball Super Star.* New York: H. Z. Walck, 1977.

Seaver, Tom, with Malky Drucker. *Tom Seaver: Portrait of a Pitcher.* New York: Holiday House, 1975.

Seaver, Tom, and Steve Jacobsen. *Baseball Is My Life.* New York: Scholastic, 1973.

———. *Pitching with Tom Seaver.* Englewood Cliffs, NJ: Prentice Hall, 1973.

Seaver, Tom, with Dick Schaap. *The Perfect Game: Tom Seaver and the Mets.* New York: Dutton, 1970

INDEX

PICTURE CREDITS
AP/Wide World Photos: pp. 2, 13, 33, 56, 58; AP/Wide World Photos, print courtesy National Baseball Library, Cooperstown, NY: p. 23; Courtesy Fresno City College: p. 19; National Baseball Library, Cooperstown, NY: p. 60; UPI/Bettmann: pp. 8, 11, 14, 20, 26, 28, 30, 35, 36, 39, 41, 42, 44, 49, 50, 53, 55.

NORMAN L. MACHT was a minor league general manager with the Milwaukee Braves and Baltimore Orioles organizations and has been a stockbroker and college professor. His work has appeared in *The Ballplayers*, the *Sporting News, Baseball Digest, USA Today, Baseball Weekly*, and *Sports Heritage*, and he is the coauthor with Dick Bartell of *Rowdy Richard* and with Rex Barney of *THANK Youuuu for Fifty Years of Baseball*. Norman Macht lives in Newark, Delaware.

JIM MURRAY, veteran sports columnist of the *Los Angeles Times*, is one of America's most acclaimed writers. He has been named "America's Best Sportswriter" by the National Association of Sportscasters and Sportswriters 14 times, was awarded the Red Smith Award, and was twice winner of the National Headliner Award. In addition, he was awarded the J. G. Taylor Spink Award in 1987 for "meritorious contributions to baseball writing." With this award came his 1988 induction into the National Baseball Hall of Fame in Cooperstown, New York. In 1990, Jim Murray was awarded the Pulitzer Prize for Commentary.

EARL WEAVER is the winningest manager in the Baltimore Orioles' history by a wide margin. He compiled 1,480 victories in his 17 years at the helm. After managing eight different minor league teams, he was given the chance to lead the Orioles in 1968. Under his leadership the Orioles finished lower than second place in the American League East only four times in 17 years. One of only 12 managers in big league history to have managed in four or more World Series, Earl was named Manager of the Year in 1979. The popular Weaver had his number, 5, retired in 1982, joining Brooks Robinson, Frank Robinson, and Jim Palmer, whose numbers were retired previously. Earl Weaver continues his association with the professional baseball scene by writing, broadcasting, and coaching.